Cliques, Phonies & Other Baloney

Trevor Romain & Elizabeth Verdick

Illustrated by Steve Mark

free spirit
PUBLISHING®

Library of Congress Cataloging-in-Publication Data
Names: Romain, Trevor, author. | Verdick, Elizabeth, author. | Mark, Steve, illustrator.
Title: Cliques, phonies & other baloney / by Trevor Romain & Elizabeth Verdick ; illustrated by Steve Mark.
Other titles: Cliques, phonies, and other baloney
Description: Revised & updated edition. | Minneapolis, MN : Free Spirit Publishing Inc., [2018] | Series: Laugh & learn | Includes index. | Identifiers: LCCN 2017041579 (print) | LCCN 2017048709 (ebook) | ISBN 9781631982439 (Web PDF) | ISBN 9781631982446 (ePub) | ISBN 9781631982422 (pbk.) | ISBN 1631982427 (pbk.)
Subjects: LCSH: Interpersonal relations in children—Juvenile literature. | Cliques (Sociology)—Juvenile literature. | Friendship in children—Juvenile literature.
Classification: LCC BF723.I646 (ebook) | LCC BF723.I646 R65 2018 (print) | DDC 155.4/1925—dc23
LC record available at https://lccn.loc.gov/2017041579

Reading Level Grade 5; Interest Level Ages 8–13;
Fountas & Pinnell Guided Reading Level T

Edited by Eric Braun
Cover and interior design by Emily Dyer
Illustrations by Steve Mark

10 9 8 7 6 5 4 3 2 1
Printed in the United States of America
V20300318

Free Spirit Publishing Inc.
6325 Sandburg Road, Suite 100
Minneapolis, MN 55427–3674
(612) 338-2068
help4kids@freespirit.com
www.freespirit.com

A wise person once said this. Maybe Oscar Wilde, maybe Thomas Merton, no one knows for sure. But from now on, you can say it and sound really,

really

smart.

Contents

Why You Need This Book (No Baloney)

Clique: It's a word that's spelled funny and sounds funny and (like a vampire) can be a pain in the neck. The word *clique* sounds like *trick*. It's tricky being "cliquey" as you go through school.

Here's one definition:

> **CLIQUE** (noun): a narrow, *exclusive* group of people—especially one held together by common interests and views.

Exclusive means having the power to *exclude* certain people, or keep them out. So, cliques like slamming the door on others. BANG!

Cliques can make you feel:

SHUT OUT

SCARED

lonely

worried

angry

unwelcome

unhappy

unpopular

PRESSURED

Any of those feelings make it harder for you to have fun, pay attention in school, or be confident about who you are.

If you're bothered by cliques, this book is for you. If you're dying to be in a clique, this book is for you, too. Even if you're in a clique, you can learn something from this book.

This book is about what cliques are, what they do, and what *you* can do about *them*. It's also about making friends—those important people in your life who don't mind if you act goofy or make mistakes. You'll learn that having good friends isn't always the same thing as being popular or being in a clique. You'll also discover that the best way to get along with people—at school or anywhere else—is to be friendly and respectful.

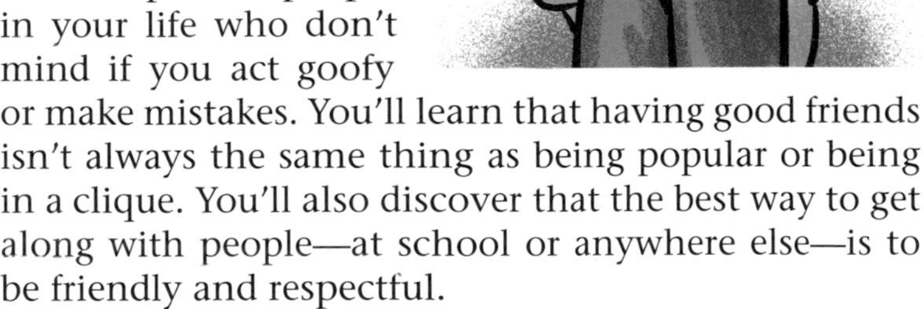

Best of all, you'll see that being yourself—not someone else—can help you grow up with greater confidence.

Chapter 1

Are You Sick of Cliques?

Does a clique at your school leave you feeling annoyed, uneasy, and a little queasy?

If cliques make you sick, you might have **cliques vomititus**, otherwise known as the clique sickness. Maybe you feel like throwing up because a clique is being cliquey. This means clique members:

1. Leave out other kids on purpose.
2. Act like they're better than everyone else.
3. Set rules or standards about how others "should" dress, behave, or be.

Clique sickness might make you want to skip school. It's hard to get out of bed and face another day of feeling like you don't belong. But each new day is a chance to kick that sickness. It may help to look closer at what makes a clique a clique.

The Ins and Outs of Cliques

Remember that definition of a clique (see page 1)? An important word in it is *exclusive*. A clique *excludes* others, or leaves them out.

A clique is different from a "group of friends." You may have a few close friends you hang around with. Maybe you live near each other, participate in the same sport or club, sit by each other at lunch, and share interests. Nothing wrong with that—especially if you make room for others to join in.

A clique has a different approach. Cliques are sticky—they stick together like glue. The members of the clique are almost always together. Maybe they take up a whole lunch table or block the hallway as they walk side by side in a line. The message is: "We're **IN**. You're **OUT**."

Experts say that some cliques behave like this to feel stronger and more powerful. Kids in the clique might feel better about themselves if they say, "Let's not hang out with *them*."

Think about how wild wolves form packs in the wilderness. Cliques aren't as dangerous, but the idea is the same. They stick together because there's safety in numbers. Being cliquey can make the clique *seem* secure (because being part of a group is a kind of protection).

So, are others left out because the clique members are somehow "better"?

NO!

People in cliques are not "better" or "above" or "more." People outside of cliques are just as important as anyone inside. That's the truth, even if it doesn't always *feel* true to you.

The #1 Clique Myth

Kids in cliques are the most confident, happy, and popular kids of all.

Some clique members may be confident and feel good about themselves. But others are insecure, and being part of a group makes them feel better. Kids in cliques often worry a lot about how they look, how they act, and what people think of them. (People *inside* the group and *outside* it.) That adds up to a lot of pressure! So, clique members may appear happy on the outside but feel intense pressure on the inside. That's no fun at all.

It's also a myth that kids in cliques are always popular. Actually, they may have trouble getting to know other classmates if they hang out with the same people all the time. That whole "sticking like glue" thing can get old after a while.

Another Clique Myth

Cliques are easy to spot.

Some cliques are cliquey on the internet. And that makes them sort of invisible. The people in online cliques hide behind their computer screens and spend time putting down others on social media. With the *click* of a mouse, these clique members gossip, spread rumors, make rude comments, or post hurtful words and images. To avoid this type of interaction, think carefully about what you do when you're online. Don't use social media sites without your parents' permission, and be sure to use the privacy settings available. Think hard about what you post or how you respond to others. Never share your passwords, even with your BFF. That's just part of staying safe online.

Weird Things Cliques Do

#1: They always travel in a group. They go everywhere together, like a herd of cows.

Why do they want to behave like an animal that spends eight hours a day "chewing its cud"? (Barfing up grass and then swallowing it again.)

#2: Cliques have rules. The rules say who's cool and who's not, and what members can and can't do.

Some of the rules are really stupid. For example, maybe kids in the clique start pressuring each other to smoke or drink alcohol. Maybe they bully others. Maybe clique members make each other tell personal secrets. Maybe they laugh at each other's mistakes or call each other out for trying to make new friends. Who needs *extra* rules—especially ones that make you feel bad?

#3: They have leaders. The leaders make rules that everyone has to follow (no matter how dumb those rules are).

Aren't people in cliques too old for Follow the Leader?

#4: They have a dress code. Most people in the clique wear the same kinds of shoes, T-shirts, jeans, jackets, and caps.

They might have to wear sneakers so big they look like snow boots.

Try this out: Say the word "clique" to yourself ten times fast. You sound like a machine or a robot. *Hmmmm*—what does that tell you?

You're not a robot. You're not a cow or a sheep that has to follow the herd. You're not some cookie-cutter person who has to be just like all the other snickerdoodles. You're **YOU**! You can learn not to get caught up in cliques. You can make friends and *be* a good friend. Keep reading to find out more.

Chapter 2

Why Do Cliques Exist?

Some cliques act like they **RULE** the SCHOOL. (Or the neighborhood. Or the mall. Or the basketball court. Or social media.) Maybe they pick on certain people or **treat them like dirt**. Maybe they even treat *you* that way.

Why does this happen? Is it because cliques are full of mean, nasty, horrible people? (Not really.) Is it because their main goal in life is to make you miserable? (Nope.)

To understand cliques, you have to know why they exist. Figuring out the *why* can make things easier to understand.

Cliques exist because everyone, no matter what age, wants to have friends. People like to feel as if they *belong*. That's human nature. Being part of a group helps us feel safe, secure, and positive.

Strange But True

People will do the **strangest** things to belong or fit in. Take Trevor, for example. When Trevor was in eighth grade, he wanted to join the "smoking clique" in the worst way. He thought those people were cool and tough, and he wanted to hang out with them. So he tried smoking once and nearly barfed. He learned that smoking cigarettes wasn't a good way to make friends.

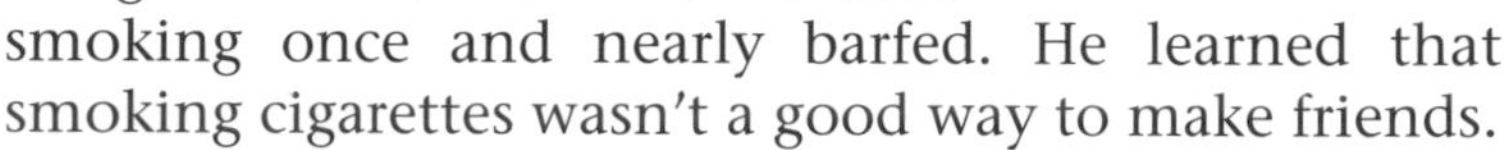

Next, he decided to jump around and act silly to get his classmates to notice him. This turned into a disaster when his pants fell down in front of a whole group of people! He realized that being a fool isn't cool, either.

Another way Trevor tried to make friends and fit in was by pretending his family was really rich. He told a group of kids at school that he lived in a mansion with an Olympic-sized, heated pool because he wanted them to think he was important. Everyone was impressed, until the group paid him a surprise visit. Trevor lived in a small house, and the closest thing to a swimming pool in his yard was a birdbath. He felt bad when the other kids learned the truth. He had pretended to be what he thought they *wanted* him to be. In the end, he realized he was just being phony.

Elizabeth also had plenty of run-ins with cliques in middle school. She changed her hair, her clothes, her shoes, her music choices, her attitude—all to be like the girls in a big clique. She even changed her handwriting! It took her three times as long to write anything because of that. Not helpful during test time . . .

Were all these changes worth it? For a couple months, Elizabeth thought they were. Then she realized she didn't really like the girls in the clique—and she didn't like *herself* while part of it. And the truth was, the girls in the clique didn't want to be her friend unless she looked and acted like them. **Guess what?** It felt *good* to go back to her old familiar handwriting and to listen to the music she loved.

Did you figure out that Trevor and Elizabeth are the authors of this book? That's right—these are our experiences with cliques, and they are the reasons we wrote this book.

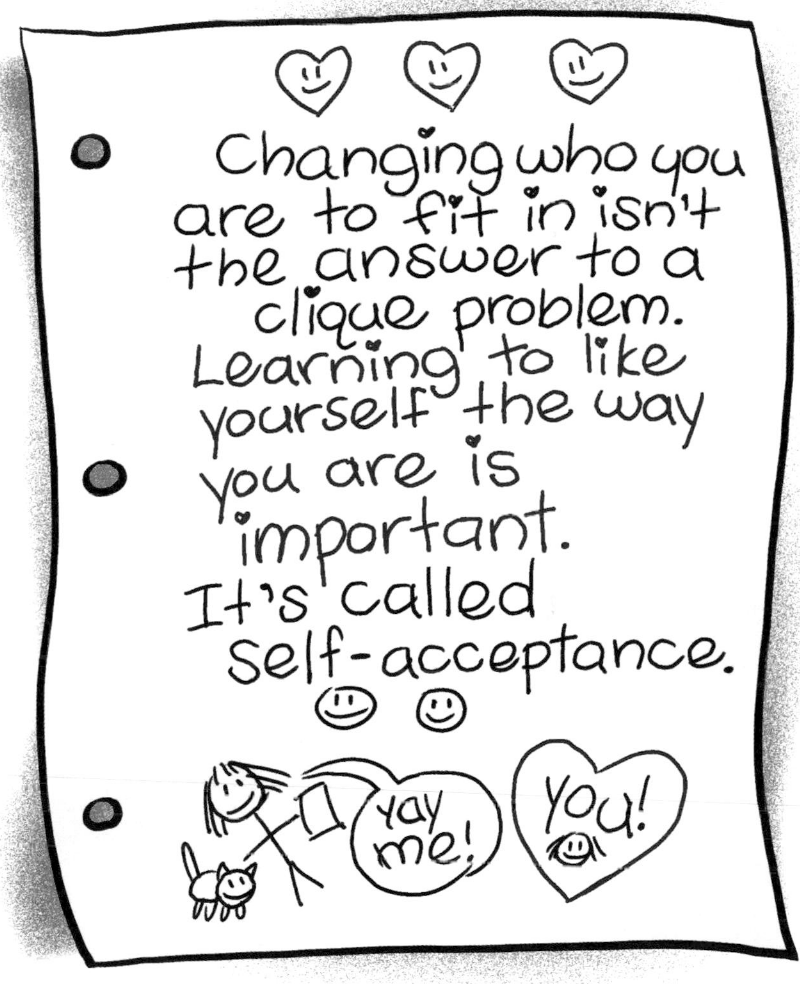

Cliques Have *Always* Been a Pain

Look at the adults in your life: They've had to face cliques just like you have. (The main difference is the clothes cliques wore back then.)

Ask the grown-ups you know about their experiences with cliques. You could talk to a parent, an adult relative, a teacher, or even your principal. It's almost guaranteed that these people dealt with cliques when they were younger. You'll see that at some point, most grown-ups tried to act a certain way or change themselves to fit in.

Changing yourself to be part of a group may work for a little while. But in the process, you can lose track of who you really are. It's like you wake up every day, thinking: *What are the rules again? How do I act? Is this right? Is this okay?* **Accckkkk, help!!!**

You're not on an alien planet. But it can feel that way when you don't know who you really are or how you want to be.

All that stress about fitting in is why some kids are in cliques (or keep looking for ways to get into one). A lot of times, kids just want to blend in. They're there, but they're more like the background instead of individual people—and that's a form of protection.

Chapter 3

Being Phony Is Baloney

What is *phony*?

No, not this:

Phony is when someone is being fake. When someone isn't the "real thing." If you see someone act, talk, dress, or behave in a certain way just to go along with the crowd (or clique), the person is probably being phony.

There once was a girl who pretended she played guitar in a band, even though she knew nothing about the guitar. She tried hard to be cool—she wore long earrings, black clothes, and dark sunglasses (even indoors).

One day, the group she hung out with asked her to play guitar for them, and she had to make up an excuse. She acted like her finger was sprained, and she walked around with a bandaged finger for three weeks to fool everyone. The day she took off the bandage, her friends asked her to join their band. What could she do but tell the truth? She was embarrassed and felt fake.

How to Spot Someone Being Phony

When people are being phony, they . . .

Pretend to be someone they're not.
Have an image to uphold.
Only care about impressing others.
Need lots of approval.
YUCK!

Phony people are easy to recognize. They stick out like blue M&M's on a double-cheese pizza.

Do *You* Act Phony? A Quiz

1. Do you put on an act to make people think you're cool?

   ☐ **yes** ☐ **no**

2. Do you tell people what you think they want to hear even if you don't mean it?

   ☐ **yes** ☐ **no**

3. Will you do almost anything just to be liked?

   ☐ **yes** ☐ **no**

4. Do you make up lies to impress people?

   ☐ **yes** ☐ **no**

5. Are you being honest on this quiz?

   ☐ **yes** ☐ **no**

Did you answer yes to any of the questions on the quiz? Then you're not being the **TRUE YOU**. If you worry about showing the world who you really are, you're not alone. Lots of kids feel the same way.

If you're being phony or fake, it may be because you think it's a way to fit in or be accepted by a clique. But why pretend to be someone else? Being fake is like wearing a mask all the time. It can get uncomfortable in there.

I
bearded
dragons

Being Yourself

To be yourself, you have to *know* yourself. It also helps to *like* yourself. Lots of people spend a lifetime learning to like who they are and not doubt themselves. You can get a head start on self-acceptance by beginning now.

If you like who you are, you'll feel more self-confident. When you're confident, it shows. You can look people in the eye, hold your head high, and speak your mind. You feel good inside and out. Best of all, people will like you for **you**.

Make a get-to-know-yourself list. Use the following questions as a guideline. When you answer the questions, don't think about what your friends or classmates might say. Or what your parents might want for you. Just answer from the heart and learn more about yourself.

Now ask yourself: *Am I doing the things I love? Do I spend time on activities that make me feel good about who I am and what I bring to the world? Who else likes doing what I do? Who can I share these activities with?*

When you find other people who like to do the same things as you, it's double the fun. Or triple—or quadruple. A feeling of belonging will follow.

And you can leave all that PHONY BALONEY behind.

Chapter 4

True Friends Rule!

Kids who have solid friendships feel better about themselves and are happier than kids who don't. That's because friends offer help and support. Friends are good to talk to, and they're fun to be around.

When somebody else likes you, it's easier for **YOU** to like you, and the world becomes a nicer place to be in.

Are Your Friendships the Real Deal?

Real friends like the *real* you. You don't have to impress them or be phony around them. That's the great thing about friends.

Real friends accept you as you are. They're there for you when you're upset or have a problem. They keep your secrets and know what makes you laugh. Best of all, they *care* about you, and you care about them.

There's no magic number of friends that is "right" or that will make you "cool." Are you the kind of person who likes to be very close to a few friends—or do you like big groups where you know a lot of people? There aren't any rules about how many friends it takes to be happy.

- You can have a best friend (or two).
- You can have siblings, cousins, or other relatives who are also your friends.
- You can have a handful of close friends.
- You can have friends who live far away that you contact mostly through social media.

- You can have groups of friends you see in familiar places (at school, on the field, at your place of worship, in your neighborhood, at Scouts, or through a volunteer program).

- You can have furry friends—or ones with feathers or fins or scales.

Friends vs. Cliques

Is there a difference between a group of friends and a clique? There can be. Take a look at some of the things cliques and groups of friends have in common. Being part of a clique or a friendship group can:

- Help you learn to get along with others
- Give you a chance to do projects together, be social, and have fun
- Help you become close to other kids, learn about each other, and trust each other

BUT (and it's a really *BIG* but) . . .

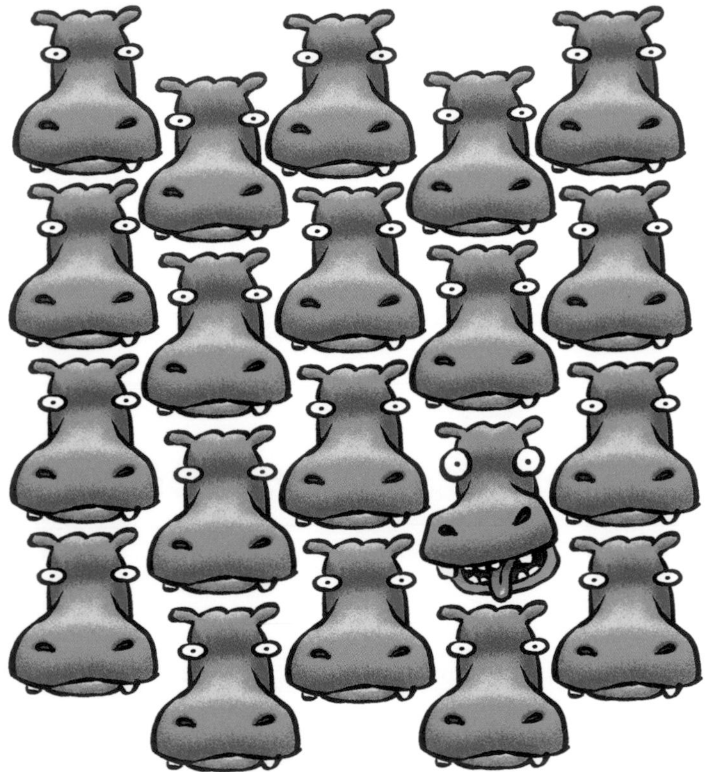

The difference is that cliques tend to make members *conform*. This means you might have to think, act, talk, and dress like everyone else in the clique. The result? You might feel phony—acting the way other people *expect*—instead of being yourself.

And remember: Cliques *exclude* people, or leave them out. The clique or its leaders decide who's allowed in and who isn't. Kids may be excluded for all kinds of reasons (none of them good ones).

Reasons like these:

race

ethnicity

RELIGIOUS BELIEFS

appearance

family

heritage

disability

size/weight

sexual or gender identity

FINANCIAL SITUATION

politics

where they live

performance in sports or competitions

name

clothes/shoes/electronics

age

HABITS

grades

INTERESTS

how "new" they are to the school, neighborhood, or community

It never feels good to be excluded for *any* reason. And the truth is, even ADULTS exclude others for such things! Leaving others out to make yourself feel better is a bad habit that can last a lifetime.

Being excluded hurts. It hurts if *you're* the one being excluded—but also if you're in a group and you see other kids being left out. You probably notice the painful feelings that exclusion can cause. And deep down, you know it's not right to disrespect others.

If you're being excluded, find kids who include you and like you for all your qualities. Start your own club or group based on **inclusion**. Welcome others. See how it grows.

Are You Hanging Out with the Wrong People?

Ask yourself these questions:

- Do I feel like I have to behave a certain way to be accepted?
- Do I feel like a fake?
- Does the group discourage me from making other friends?
- Does it seem like I always have to meet the approval of others in the group?
- Do I feel out of place with these people?

If you answered *yes* to any of these questions, you might want to think about finding other friends. You can work on forming a new friendship circle with kids who let you just be you—also known as *real* friends.

Sometimes kids join a clique because they are more comfortable being "followers" than "leaders." For a while, it might seem easier to let others take the lead. But what if clique leaders encourage you to be rude or mean? What if they boss you around? What if you decide you don't want to follow along after all?

Remember that you're not "employed" by the clique. It's not your job to follow orders from them! You can make your own choices. You can find new friends. (For tips on getting out of a clique, see page 90.)

Friendship Pointers

If you want new friends (or more friends), all you have to do is look. Your friends don't need to go to the same school as you. They don't have to be the same age, gender, or race as you. Your friend can be a kid who's in a grade above or below yours, or even an elderly neighbor. Your friend can be a boy or girl. You'd be amazed by how much you can learn from people who aren't just like you.

Friendships don't just happen. It takes effort on your part to make friends and keep them. In fact, being a friend is something you can work on a little bit each day.

Do's and Don'ts for Making Friends

DO talk to people. If you're shy at first, just say something friendly like, "Your new backpack is cool." Or ask a question like, "Do you know what tonight's homework is?" With practice, starting a conversation will get easier.

DON'T stay inside by yourself all day watching TV, picking your nose, playing video games, staring at your phone, or sitting in front of the computer. You won't meet any new people, and a spider might build a web on your head.

DO try to make other people feel good. Ask questions to show you're interested in them. You can try something like, "I noticed you're really good at art. Do you have some drawings you could show me sometime?" Offer compliments such as, "Nice catch," or "You were so smart in class today."

DON'T walk up to someone and say something like, "Be my friend or you'll be sorry!" You can't force someone to be friends with you.

DO invite people to join you. Ask other kids to hang out with you, invite someone to sit with you at lunch, or start a club and find out if other people want to join. Invite someone to text or be friends online. This will help people get to know you better.

DON'T invite your whole class over for an all-you-can-eat pizza party, order 35 pepperoni pizzas on your mom's credit card, and feed the leftovers to the cat. This could get you in big trouble.

DO be a good listener. If you're the one doing all the talking, chances are you're boring somebody (maybe even yourself). To be a good listener, you have to really *listen* to other people and *hear* what they say. Look the person in the eye and nod your head to show you understand.

DON'T brag about yourself, hog the spotlight, or show off—and then, when everyone ignores you, turn up the volume and talk even LOUDER. You'll only drive people away.

DO talk to the "new kid." If you've ever moved to a new neighborhood or gone to a different school, you know how it feels to be new (lonely, strange, and scary). Make an effort to get to know new kids, and they'll probably like you right away. Show them around school or the neighborhood, sit with them at lunch, and introduce them to other people you know.

DON'T overdo it. (There's such a thing as being *too* friendly.) If you get right in the new person's face and say: "Hi! I'd really like to be your friend because you're new here, and I think you look like a really nice person, and I need a friend right now, and blah, blah, blah, and . . . " you're saying too much too fast. If you notice spit flying out of your mouth, take a deep breath and slow down.

DO include people. Remember, cliques tend to leave people out. They're picky about who can hang around with them. It's much more friendly to *include* people in social situations—even if you don't know them well, and even if they're different from you.

DON'T walk around calling people losers, jerks, dopes, nerds, dunderheads, dweebs, wimps, or other names—in person or online. It's not a friendly or nice thing to do. Plus, you'll probably get a reputation as someone to avoid.

Here's a really **BIG** tip for making friends:

Six Ways to Be Friendly

#1: Smile! It's better than walking around with a scowl on your face.

#2: Say hi to people in the hall and in class—even if you don't know them very well.

At first, you might get some funny looks (like, "Do I *know* this person?"), but soon everyone will realize you're just being friendly.

#3: Compliment at least one person each day. Just don't say something like, "Wow, your hair looks really good—for a change." Make sure the compliment is something you really like about the person.

#4: Be a good sport about losing a game or any other competition. It's much more friendly than stomping off while shouting at the top of your lungs, "I can't believe those losers won!"

#5: Talk to people before or after class, or when you're at your locker, waiting for the bus, or in line. Each person you talk to is a potential friend.

TIP: Avoid talking to people *during* class. Teachers hate that.

#6: Be kind online. Only post stuff that's *positive*. Don't use social media to send rude messages or images. And don't participate in mean polls or chats. Stick up for friends—and yourself—online.

What does all this add up to? Good people skills. Having good people skills means being cheerful, kind, positive, generous, or funny.

You can polish your people skills, if you want to. How? Smile at everyone you meet, laugh a lot, show your confidence, be kind to your classmates, listen to your teachers, and don't be afraid to be you. You'll attract new friends. You'll seem all-around friendly. Maybe you'll even become . . .

A PEOPLE MAGNET.

Chapter 5

Is Popularity Important?

Many kids want to be popular more than anything else. Have you ever thought:

- "I wish I were popular."
- "If I were popular, I'd be happy."
- "So-and-so is a lot more popular than I am."
- "My life would be so much better if I were popular!"

The Truth About Popularity

Being popular can be fun. You might feel important and well-liked. Popularity can make you feel like you belong and have lots of fun things to do.

But many kids think popularity is *way* more important than it is. Here are just a few things that are more important:

- your family
- your true friends
- your schoolwork
- your hobbies, activities, and interests
- your pet
- your goals and dreams
- how you take care of yourself and others
- and, most of all, your opinion of yourself

Want to hear some **top-secret**, surprising, shocking news?! (Turn the page.)

When people wish to be popular, often what they really want is to feel good about themselves.

Maybe you think the popular kids are the coolest people on the planet. Maybe you believe you're a big nobody. Not true! You're a unique individual with a lot to offer the world. You just need to tell yourself that . . . and believe it.*

*If it's hard for you to believe this, check out some ways to think positive about yourself on page 74.

Popularity Pop Quiz

True or false? The popular kids are always:

1. The best looking

2. The best dressed
3. The most athletic
4. The happiest

5. The strongest
6. The richest
7. The coolest
8. The most talented

9. The smartest
10. The ones with the best stuff

Answers: **1.** false | **2.** false | **3.** false | **4.** false | **5.** false
6. false | **7.** false | **8.** false | **9.** false | **10.** false.

Some of the popular kids you know may be good-looking, good at sports, well-dressed, and more, but these qualities don't *guarantee* popularity.

It's not only what's on the outside that counts. What's *inside* matters much more. Here are some inner qualities that give a person true worth:

kindness

honesty

curiosity

intelligence

RESPECT FOR OTHERS

integrity

generosity

humor

caring about others

being open and welcoming

Think Positive (About Yourself)

Do you spend time worrying about whether you're popular? Do you often tell yourself that other kids are better than you? Stop! Halt!

CUT IT OUT!

Instead, focus on feeling good about yourself. With practice, you can turn your negative thoughts into positive ones. Try this:

Instead of:

Tell yourself:

"I have friends who really care about me. That's more important than trying to make *everybody* like me."

Two Popularity Myths

Popular people are better than everyone else.

HOGWASH!

TOTALLY UNTRUE!

NONSENSE!

RUBBISH!

Popular people aren't better than everyone else. Kids who are popular are still human—they have problems, hopes, dreams, worries, fears, good days, and bad days just like other people do.

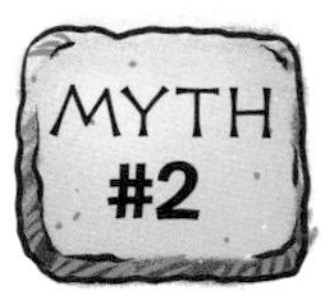

MYTH #2 **To be popular, you need to treat some kids badly.**

BALONEY!

Popularity isn't about making other people feel *unpopular*. And it's not about telling other kids they're not good enough to hang around you. You can be popular *and* a nice person at the same time.

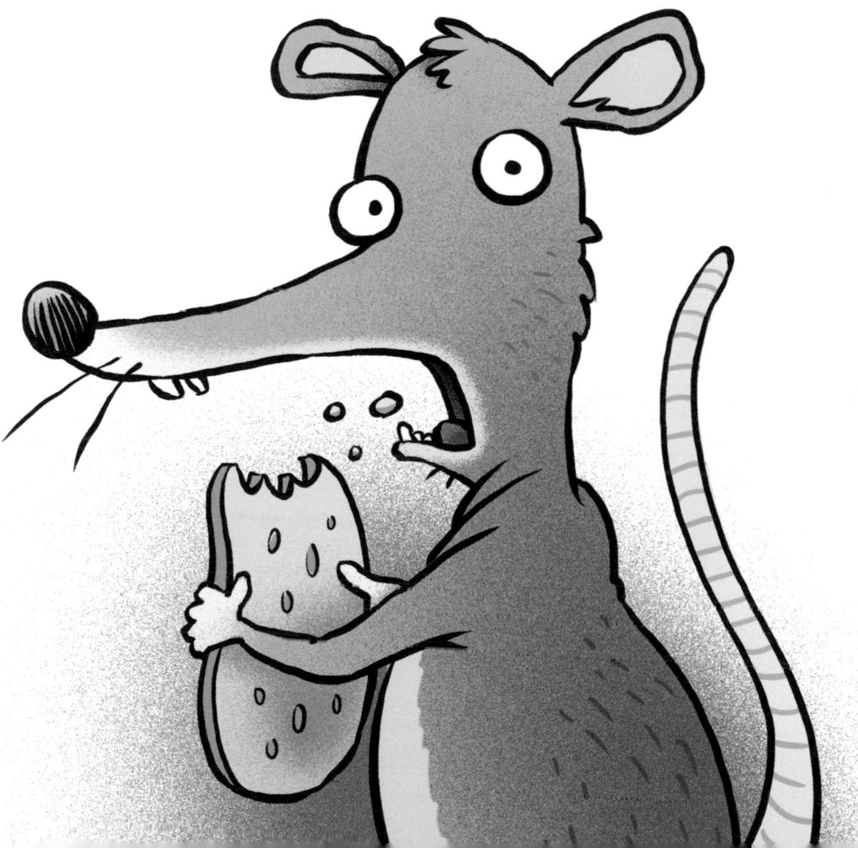

A Question for You

Are you popular with yourself? (Don't worry, this isn't a trick question.)

If you base your self-image on what *other* people think of you, instead of what *you* think of you, you'll always feel like you don't measure up. Or you'll spend a lot of time trying to please everyone. Either way, you're being too hard on yourself.

A Few Words of Advice

- Be yourself.
- Learn to like yourself.
- Be kind to other people.

That's the *real* secret to being a person who others look up to and care about. Popularity is optional.

Chapter 6

When Cliques Are Bad News for Good People

What do cliques and popularity have in common? Many kids want to be popular or in a clique because *the need to belong* is so strong. They want to be accepted, approved of, and admired. (Maybe this is how you feel most of the time.) It's perfectly normal to want to belong. Everyone does, on some level.

But what happens when the **IN** crowd leaves you **OUT**? Or what if no matter how friendly you are, a clique decides to snub you or tries to make you feel bad about yourself?

Uh-oh, you're dealing with a **CLIQUE**. And that's **NO GOOD**!

The Phony Times
Clique Rejects Good Person

Cliques Are Bad News

A clique can *really* make you sick. You might feel queasy (like you just ate too much candy) or scared (like you have a big math test that—YIKES!—you forgot to study for).

You might even feel like doing something mean and nasty—something that might make the clique feel as rotten as you do.

HELPFUL HINT:

This is a *verrrry* bad idea.

The Four Worst Tricks for Dealing with Bad Cliques

These are all great ideas . . . if you want to make things worse. **Don't try them!** Later in this chapter you'll find smarter ways to deal with a clique that makes you sick.

#1: Ignoring the clique. That's like cleaning your room by cramming your stuff in your closet and slamming the door shut. Sooner or later, you have to open the door—WHOA! LOOK OUT! You'll feel better if you face your problems instead of pretending they don't exist.

#2: Getting back at the clique. Don't launch a spoonful of peas at the "popular" lunch table. This will only make people mad at you.

#3: Making enemies of the clique. If you try to threaten or embarrass the clique members, you might end up as a moving target, running for cover in the school hallways. (Then you'll feel even *more* sick when you have to go to school.)

And if you try to get revenge on the clique through social media, that can backfire, too. You may feel "anonymous" on social media, but it's not safe to post nasty messages or spread hate online. You'll likely be found out. And there will probably be consequences at home and at school.

#4: Being phony to impress the clique. People can smell phoniness a mile away. It's better just to be yourself.

So, What *Should* You Do?

Don't let a bad clique spoil a perfectly good day!

If you're on the outs with a clique or with the popular crowd, you may feel sad and rejected. But you *do* have a choice for handling the situation. (No, you don't have to pack your bags and move to the North Pole!)

You can . . .

DARE TO BE DIFFERENT.

Hi.

Being Different Is Okay

Being different doesn't mean you're weird, strange, or unpopular. It means you're an independent thinker—an individual. It means you're a very interesting, creative, thoughtful, worthwhile person . . . with or without a crowd.

How do you learn to be an individual? Start by believing in yourself. Find your strengths and make the most of them. Maybe you're an artist, a joke teller, a helper, a dreamer, an animal lover, a reader, or someone who likes being in the great outdoors. What quality of yours can help you gain confidence and reach out to others? What plans can you make to share who you are with other kids?

TIP: If you want to make people laugh, you can tell jokes or funny stories. Just make sure you're laughing *with* people, not *at* them. And don't be afraid to laugh at yourself.

Reach out in positive ways: talk face-to-face, write nice notes, be friendly online, invite people to sit near you at school, include others in games, sports, and outdoor activities.

You can also get involved with other kids who seem fun and interesting—even if they're outside of your school. Join a team, be a Girl Scout or Boy Scout, find a community club, join the youth group at your place of worship, or become a volunteer. When you're involved in lots of activities, you have a better chance of meeting people and learning new things about yourself.

Tips for Kissing a Clique Goodbye

Sometimes, kids feel a need to leave their clique. It's kind of like a breakup. Breakups aren't easy, but you *can* move on.

You don't have to make an announcement over the loudspeaker—or broadcast on social media. Start by looking for ways to be friendly to others outside the group. If clique members pressure you to *only* be friends with those on their imaginary "approved list," you can say, "I can make my own choices." This takes courage. Dig deep! If you need extra support during this time, talk to your parents, teachers, or school counselor.

I am leaving this clique now!
EXIT

Fill your time with new activities so you have something positive to do. Join a sport, a club, or an activity; take lessons; spend time at your library or community center; invite someone over; say *yes* if someone invites you. Having a full schedule means you won't have as much time with the clique. Eventually, the members of the clique will see you've moved on.

Thanks for inviting me over.

Beware of cliques using social network sites to influence you. Don't respond to online dissing, rumors, or gossip. Only post profile information and photos that you want everyone to see—what goes online *stays* online. Keep your messages private. Avoid getting caught up in cyberbullying (bullying that takes place online, in texts, and through other media). If you're a victim of bullying, teasing, or hurtful behavior, talk to adults you trust.

Delete.
Delete!

Friendship Matters

Remember, you always have choices about your friendships. You can find other kids to hang out with if a clique doesn't want you—or if you don't want the clique. You can decide that being popular with your *friends* is the only popularity that really matters. It's up to you.

If you have one or two good friends, that's great! But you don't have to stop there. Use your people skills to make a few more friends throughout middle school and beyond. After all, it's nice to have people who care about you and like you for who you are.

The Top 10 Ways to Keep Your Friends

10. Show them kindness and respect.
9. Stick up for them.
8. If you make a promise, keep it.
7. Tell the truth (but be kind about it).
6. Be supportive when your friends need help or advice.

5. Work on your friendships by listening, spending time together, and being supportive. Otherwise your friends might feel neglected.

4. Don't try to change your friends—accept them the way they are.

3. Treat your friends the way you want them to treat you.

2. If you hurt a friend, say you're sorry.

1. If a friend hurts you and apologizes, accept the apology.

And one more thing:

You guys are awesome.

Read More About It

KidsHealth: "How Cliques Make Kids Feel Left Out"
kidshealth.org/en/kids/clique.html
Learn what cliques are, why they can be hurtful for people outside them *and* inside them, and what you can do to feel better. You'll also find links to related articles on bullying, gossip, peer pressure, and more.

Stick Up for Yourself! by Gershen Kaufman, Lev Raphael, and Pamela Espeland. Free Spirit Publishing, 1999. This classic resource offers help for any kid who's ever been picked on at school, bossed around, blamed for things he or she didn't do, or treated unfairly.

The Survival Guide for Making and Being Friends by James J. Crist. Free Spirit Publishing, 2014. This straightforward handbook for kids includes practical advice for everything from breaking the ice, to developing friendships, to overcoming problems.

The Worst-Case Scenario Survival Handbook: Middle School by David Borgenicht, Ben H. Winters, and Robin Epstein. Chronicle Books, 2009. Get humorous but true-to-life advice for tackling all sorts of middle school mishaps, like how to handle the cold shoulder from a newly too-cool buddy, how to stop a rumor in its tracks, and how to be *truly* popular.

Index

About the Authors and Illustrator

Trevor Romain is an award-winning author and illustrator as well as a sought-after motivational speaker. His books have sold more than a million copies and have been published in 18 languages. For more than 20 years, Trevor has traveled throughout the world, speaking to thousands of school-age children. Trevor is well-known for his work with the Make-A-Wish Foundation, the United Nations, UNICEF, USO, and the Comfort Crew for Military Kids, which he cofounded. Trevor lives in Austin, Texas.

Elizabeth Verdick has written children's books for all ages, from toddlers to teens. She has worked with Trevor on many titles in the Laugh & Learn series. Elizabeth loves helping kids through her work as a writer and an editor. She lives in Minnesota with her husband and their two (nearly grown) children, and she plays traffic cop for their many furry, four-footed friends.

Steve Mark is a freelance illustrator and a part-time puppeteer. He lives in Minnesota and is the father of three and the husband of one. Steve has illustrated all the books in the Laugh & Learn series, including *Don't Behave Like You Live in a Cave* and *Bullying Is a Pain in the Brain.*

Free Spirit's Laugh & Learn® Series

Solid information, a kid-centric point of view, and a sense of humor combine to make each book in our Laugh & Learn series an invaluable tool for getting through life's rough spots. For ages 8–13. *Paperback; 80–136 pp.; illust.; 5⅛" x 7"*

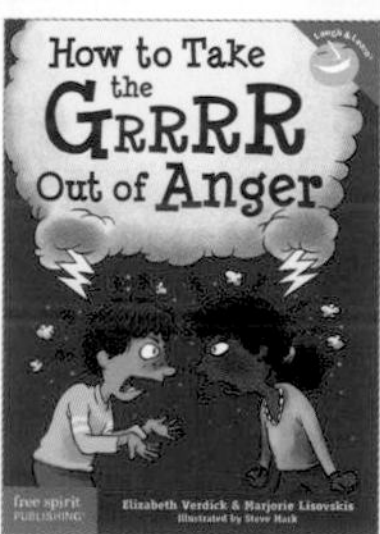

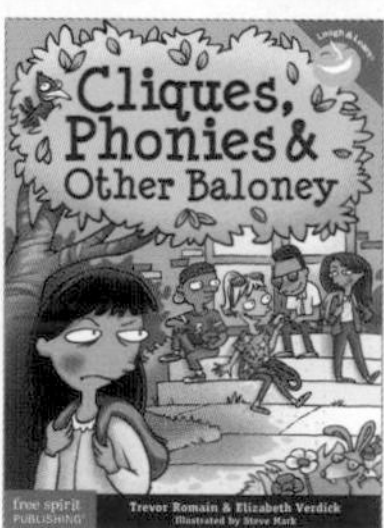

Interested in purchasing multiple quantities and receiving volume discounts?
Contact edsales@freespirit.com or call 1.800.735.7323 and ask for Education Sales.

Many Free Spirit authors are available for speaking engagements, workshops, and keynotes. Contact speakers@freespirit.com or call 1.800.735.7323.

www.freespirit.com